MW00721174

Teaching The Mystery Of God To Children

A Book Of Clues

Judy Gattis Smith

CSS Publishing Company, Inc., Lima, Ohio

TEACHING THE MYSTERY OF GOD TO CHILDREN

Copyright © 2005 by
CSS Publishing Company, Inc.
Lima, Ohio

Some scripture quotations are from the New Revised Standard Version of the Bible, copyright 1989 by the Division of Christian Education of the National Council of the Churches of Christ in the USA. Used by permission.

Some scripture quotations are from the Holy Bible, New International Version. Copyright © 1973, 1978, 1984 International Bible Society. Used by permission of Zondervan Bible Publishers. All rights reserved.

Library of Congress Cataloging-in-Publication Data

Smith, Judy Gattis, 1933-
    Teaching the mystery of God to children : a book of clues / Judy Gattis Smith.
        p. cm.
    ISBN 0-7880-2355-1 (alk. paper)
1. Christian education of children. I. Title.

BV1475.3.S55 2005
268'.432—dc22

2004029084

For more information about CSS Publishing Company resources, visit our website at www.csspub.com or e-mail us at custserv@csspub.com or call (800) 241-4056.

Cover design by Jenna Brannon
ISBN 0-7880-2355-1   PRINTED IN U.S.A.

Table Of Contents

Introduction

Why This Book?

I believe our children are having God encounters that we, as their teachers do not know about. Yes, our squirming, loud, sometimes exasperating students are wondering about theological questions and having experiences that they don't talk to anyone about. Maybe you thought spiritual matters were adult fare — not so.

I base this belief on two things: My own experiences as a child, and some in-depth, one-on-one conversations with adult friends who have had their own experiences.

Even now when I think about death I recall a singular incident from my childhood. I was young, probably seven or eight years of age. A group from my school had gone to a public park in mid-summer for swimming and a picnic. With taunting dares I was challenged to jump off the high diving board. I remember climbing and climbing upward — at first gleefully. As I neared the top of the ladder it seemed to sway. I held on tight and continued climbing. When I stepped on the board it was springy under my feet. It felt wobbly. My arms thrashed about. There was no support. I was terrified. All I wanted to do was climb back down the ladder but others had pushed behind me waiting their turn. There was no going back the way I had come. I crept to the edge and was almost overcome with vertigo when looking down. I don't remember what finally impelled me to jump, but the fall downward was swift. The water surrounding me at the bottom was a beautiful transparent blue-green and the force of the jump shot me straight upward like a rocket. It was glorious! I was blessed with an overwhelming sense of presence. Then I heard an inner voice say: "Death is like this." Over the years the symbolism in the experience has taken on increasing meaning but the strong, comforting assurance of that inner voice full of so much love remains with me from childhood.

It was only recently that I have shared that experience with close friends and have been rewarded by hearing their stories —

5

stories of surrounding light in dangerous situations, of angels that came to them as young children — experiences they had when young that they never shared.

What does all this say to us as Sunday school teachers? We can't pry these experiences from our children. This might expose them to ridicule from their classmates and crush their budding spiritual lives. Dr. Robert Coles, chronicler of children's behavior said, "Now many children are ashamed of their spirituality — afraid of being mocked by the secular community, afraid others will see them as absurd, foolish, or superstitious."

But there are things we can do and this book tries to suggest some of them. We as teachers can tune ourselves to the voices of children — to listen with gentle awareness to the spiritual overtones behind the obvious questions they ask. We can try to be aware of hints that a child is seeking, with unusual interest, to understand something. We can make ourselves available for one-on-one private times to listen to a child. We can learn to affirm as valid a child's different definitions and dimensions of knowing God. We can attempt to humble ourselves to learn wonder from our children.

We can also give them content to help in understanding their experiences. We can teach the strong tenets of our faith: love, forgiveness, hope. These are also mysteries. We can give them words and stories from our faith tradition as background and bedrock for their religious experiences. We can saturate them with our sacred stories and say, over and over: "And in such ways God may speak to us again."

Send them out from your classrooms each day with this blessing, "May you see the mystery and love of God today."

I sometimes wonder what marvels of holiness we will one day discover to have been active all around us in the children in our classrooms whose inner depth we never recognized.

Who Is This Book For?

If you are a teacher of children in the church or, if you are responsible for the spiritual life of a child, this book invites you on a quest to explore the mysteries of our faith. You are invited to seek the Divine Mystery at the core of the universe.

You will be telling Bible stories, but beyond and beneath our stories is a great mystery. You will be imparting knowledge but more than knowledge is a basic human instinct for wonder and awe. You will go back to the source, dealing with ultimate questions: Who is God? How can we know God, not just know about God? Who am I? Is there meaning and purpose in life? You will explore these questions. We seek an encounter with the invisible God who is willing to be known. Our teaching will not be so much adding on as drawing out the spirituality that is already there in our students and ourselves. Our emphasis is awe not strategy.

Our children are probably familiar with a loving Jesus, a kindly Father-God but where have they learned about the Supreme, Numinous, Omnipotent, All-Powerful God of the Universe? Where have they been affirmed in their experiences of such?

And how do you teach about such a God? How do you search for answers that can be experienced but never be fully known? Perhaps the biggest question: When do you guide and when do you just get out of the way?

Our approach must be different from the traditional teaching approach. This is not a factual, informational how-to book. Here children are our guides as much as we are theirs. Instead of objects for us to educate we see children as active meaning-makers in their own ongoing story of faith and life. We take seriously children's visions and dreams, the looks from their fresh eyes.

Since there is no map for this journey we will be following clues. This is a book of clues. Together with the children we will interact, participate, and explore. Together we will attempt to broaden, deepen, and enrich our connection to the invisible God. In each Clue chapter there will be some input. One or more ideas will be suggested for you to try with your class and at the end of each chapter there will be questions for you as teacher to ponder. Children are already spiritual. We can help make it safe and normal for them to feel and express their spiritual nature. Clues are invitations.

Our purpose is not simply to give a child a set of beliefs but a vision of the wonder and immensity of God.

As You Begin

Any real teacher is only a pointing finger.
— ancient saying

It seems almost too obvious to say — an important job we have as teachers in the church is to get our students to think about God. Let me repeat, not *learn* about God — *think* about God.

This was brought vividly to my mind with a recent confirmation class. The night before being confirmed, the eighth graders went apart from the group with a copy of the vows they were to affirm the next day. Instructions were to read the vows slowly and think about them. When the group regathered one boy said, "That's the first time I've sat alone and thought about God." I was shocked. He was an eighth grader from an active church family who had attended Sunday school and vacation Bible school all his life. Yet he had never reflected upon God before.

I had forgotten the highly structured lives our children live today. If not engaging in some activity they are bombarded by a cacophony of electronic devices — blaring music — mesmerizing television images. The depths of the inner life are rarely experienced in a culture like ours, so overwhelmingly absorbed in externals. Yet, it is in silence and reflection where God is first found.

Perhaps as teachers and parents we have been afraid to encourage this exploration of God by our children. After all, if we push our minds as far as we can in explaining God, we are still only guessing. Maybe we don't want to say to our children "We just don't know." A hard truth for some of us as teachers is that we don't need to have all the answers. We must be willing to listen to children's words. Since the last word of Christian faith has not been spoken, we dare not indulge in the luxury of refusing new words, images, and symbols just because they come from children. Be honest with your students. Let the church be the place where children and youth experience adults struggling to understand the wonder and mystery of God for themselves. There is little to be gained by saying more than is known.

If our faith in God cannot be bewildered and perplexed then we have diminished God, and our faith is more in our religious system and religious jargon than in our Holy God.

One challenge for teaching in the church is to point our children to reflection — to thinking about the big picture — about consequences — about other people and their feelings — about their lives — about God. As we attempt to do this we face a problem. While on the one hand we want to affirm and encourage the spiritual side of our children, if we turn a spotlight on spiritual activity it may disappear. I learned this the hard way.

Jason was a popular, good-looking boy in my fourth grade Sunday school class. Sometimes he startled my co-teacher and me with the depth of his answers and insights. Once, because of another activity involving students in my class, Jason and I were alone. Seizing this opportunity I said, "Jason, I think you have a special understanding of God, can we talk about it?"

"Okay," he said.

I should have been more sensitive to the look on his face which spoke denial to his words. "Well, what do you think God is like?" I asked.

"I don't know."

"Have you ever thought about how God is present with us all the time?"

"I don't know."

I continued insensitively to quiz him.

When Jason crawled under the table I finally got the message. To add to my failure, Jason's comments in later classroom experiences were humorous, irreverent comments quite different from his previous insightful ones.

I learned new understanding of the phrases "nipping a flower in the bud" and "pulling the shell off a hatching chick."

Sharing spiritual growth with a child is not an easy task. Timing and sensitivity are important. Encounter with God is not something we, as teachers, can control or arrange.

And as has been true many times in my life, I learned from a child. I was making too much of Jason's statements. I was over-emphasizing in a way that was pressuring him to perform. Fortunately, Jason was too smart to fall for that. How much wiser it would have been to have been a teacher open and sensitive to Jason's leading.

Tremble at your responsibility, but be encouraged. Despite the mediocrity in most of us, it is often stunning to see the holiness God brings forth — often in our children. Is this not what keeps us teaching?

A bumper sticker that keeps me humble reads: "When I set out to edify I seek to impress and become a well-intended Pharisee."

Before we begin following our clues, begin an exploration of your own life. This section is designed to help you reflect and remember the many stories of your life experience. As you ponder these questions hidden memories may surface. You may discover your own life provides clues on this spiritual journey. There are no right or wrong answers to these questions — only the answers that work for you.

There are also reflection questions for you to consider in regards to your particular class or individual child.

A Time To Reflect

1. Do I have a set image of what a teacher in the church should do or be? Write the first three words that pop in your mind.

2. What personal traits do I have for this kind of teaching suggested in this chapter? In this private moment access your talents. Am I:
    *   Someone who pays attention
    *   Someone who is available
    *   Someone who shares delights
    *   Listens
    *   Respects
    *   Participates
    *   Loves

3. Have I ever had an experience of the numinous in my own life — a time when I felt the presence of some mysterious *other*?

4. When have I gained spiritual insight from a child? What and in what circumstances? What have I learned from children?

5. When I was a child what did I think life would be like?

6. Am I enthusiastic about the type of teaching I do?

7. Have I ever felt the presence of God in my classroom?

Clue 1
The Bible

As we begin our journey in the mystery of God we have a powerful first clue; a book to accompany us on our way. But, you say, we always use the Bible in our teaching. What is new about that?

Consider first, how we use the Bible in our teaching. Before we insist that our children see the world as we have seen it we should listen to how they may see it with fresh eyes and imaginative hearts. The Bible is unfamiliar and strange to our students in its customs and language. This very fact can work to our advantage. The Bible tells a story of otherness and awe.

Let a Bible story speak on its own of the wonders of God and new wonders will be disclosed. It is amazing how we "jazz" up Bible stories for children. In our eagerness to share the good news we fill their heads with implicit instructions: "Be sure to see *this* in the story" or "Look at it from *this* angle." We insert add-ons. We are quick to put forth examples from *our* experience. We strive to make the story fun and contemporary.

The simple story itself carries great power. It is the stories that tell us who we are as Christians and what God is like.

If you find that the stories of our religion no longer help us interpret our lives with creative meaning, try this simple experiment.

Begin with a short two verse story such as Mark 1:9-11, the baptism of Jesus, and follow these instructions:

Step 1: Have the class read the story aloud just for the entertainment of the story itself, or you read it to them as expressively as you can.

Step 2: Each member of the class then copies the story in their own handwriting, word for word. Writers attest to a certain rhythmic connection between writing something in longhand and brain work. In these days of computers this is becoming a vanishing method. Recapture this power.

Step 3: Send the class outdoors with their copied script and instruct each student to find a place to sit apart and read the story again. Instruct them to read slowly and reflect on it. If weather and situations do not permit an outdoor experience find a place indoors that allows for privacy.

Step 4: Students attempt to create a silence within themselves and let the story speak to them individually. Tell them to let the story speak to their hearts, not to their brains. Instruct them to just be quiet and live with the story. Instruct them to read as one prepared to be surprised. It may take time and practice but a child can move beyond an initial restlessness and aversion to being still.

Step 5: Give these final instructions: Carry the images and insight from the story with you through the day, praying that the story will reveal emerging truths about God and about you.

In a recent fourth grade class it was difficult to get children not to respond with the "right" answer as they had learned it but to get them to think beyond the correct response they had been taught. Over and over we would say, "This is the story. Can you think of a deeper meaning? Can it mean something special to you? If you were a character in this story what would you do? Can you help us (the teachers) understand?"

Students of any age or ability can find transformation. Every story worth telling has an inner life, the meaning of which has the power to transform. We need to let our students hear them over and over and think about them. Our task is to pose honest questions and listen to their responses.

Just as we would not offer our students fresh fruit and chew it up before we gave it to them, so, too, we need to simply present the refreshing word of God. In this way, most of the stories were originally told.

A Time To Reflect

1. As a teacher or guiding parent use this five-step method to find clues for your teaching and new insight for your life. Study Mark 10:13-16.

   People were bringing little children to Jesus to have him touch them, but the disciples rebuked them. When Jesus saw this, he was indignant. He said to them, "Let the little children come to me, and do not hinder them, for the kingdom of God belongs to such as these."

   Follow the five-step method:
   - Read aloud for enjoyment
   - Copy in longhand
   - Read story again silently
   - Let the story speak to you personally
   - Carry the story with you through the day

2. Consider Bible stories you might use in your class. Perhaps the stories suggested in your curriculum could be mined in this way. Include stories about God speaking through and to children. Read the story of young Samuel in chapter 1 (1 Samuel 3). Put yourself in the role of Eli the priest. How does Eli respond to a child's questions? How might you respond?

3. Consider Joseph in the Old Testament (Genesis 37:5-11). How did his brothers react to his visions and dreams? Recall times you have experienced when siblings or other children reacted to one child's spiritual event or story.

4. Consider Joel (Joel 2:28) who says our sons and daughters will prophesy and see visions. Meditate on this scripture. Do you believe this? Do you have you a personal example here?

As we continue to pursue how the Bible gives us clues to the mysteries of God look at some of the mind-stretching concepts in the Bible. For example, incarnation. Specifically at the Advent/ Christmas season how do you teach incarnation, that moment eternity intersected time and Christ was born?

As much as we dearly love the familiar telling of the shepherds and the manger, we know there is more to this story. There is numinous power and indescribable awe. There is mystery waiting in darkness and that mystery somehow is love. How do we make these thoughts accessible to children?

Try the route from the divine to the ridiculous.

Ask children to think about expressions they have heard illustrating overwhelming surprise. As humans struggling to annunciate our encounter with awe, we often use earthy bodily images. For example:

- Knocks your socks off
- Bowls you over
- Takes your breath away
- Makes your hair stand on end
- Sweeps you off your feet
- Staggers you
- Popeyed or eye-opening
- Blows you down
- Thunderstruck

Can the class think of others?

What are some utterances of amazement such as:

- Wow
- Holy cow
- Holy mackerel
- Holy smoke
- Will wonders never cease?

Invite the children to choose one of these expressions or one from their experience and draw it in a cartoon using the familiar Christmas characters. For example an amazed shepherd or an awestruck wise man.

This session may take a turn to "silly" but keep the children focused on overwhelming surprise. Visual images compliment words of scripture and make their meaning more powerful. God in human form. Could anything be more amazing?

A Time To Reflect

In these moments of personal meditation consider the use of humor in your teaching.

1. The Bible is a serious book about serious topics. The subject, incarnation, is one of reverence and awe pondered by scholars and theologians. Did this exercise make you feel uncomfortable?

2. Children seem born with an inherent capacity to laugh, smile, play, and generally make fun and light of life. Recall some recent times you have seen examples of this. Enjoy these memories. Jot them down to help you remember.

3. Recall experiences from your life when you have seen examples of the humorous in sacred situations. For example: gargoyles seen in medieval churches alongside angels and saints.

4. Have you ever thought of God as having a sense of humor? Why or why not?

Clue 2
Art

For our next clue let us consider art. Looking at beauty lifts our spirits and turns our thoughts to God. One author said, "Beauty teases open the heart." We hunger for visions of divine experience. Sight makes the greatest impression. When we behold something it becomes real. Just as too quick an interpretation of a Bible story cuts off questioning, too quick an explanation of art has the same effect. This may be an act of irreverence. In the presence of the sacred, sometimes the best response is an awesome silence. We stand in reverence before a painting, a flower, a rainbow, or a spectacular sunset and we experience something of the Invisible God.

A Christian educator whom I admire very much, now retired, told me this story: In her very first job she came upon some women cleaning out Sunday school rooms — tossing away papers and half-made crafts and old pictures. One picture captured her attention — a very familiar picture at that time she said. It was the picture of a young girl dressed in 1920s clothes sitting outdoors looking up at a small bird in a tree nearby. For some reason she picked this picture out of the trash can and kept it. In years of moving to other churches she always kept that picture. Now, living in a retirement home that picture still accompanies her. Once she was told it was now an antique and a dealer offered to buy it, but she says she wouldn't sell it for any amount of money. That picture speaks to her. She looked at me thoughtfully and said, "I really can't tell you why."

God comes to us in so many non-verbal forms. Art is often an avenue.

But tastes in art are individual and this is important to remember as we teach. Too often we have been too literal in our Sunday school art. In art expressions, as well as other teaching methods in the church, we often take the path of least resistance, the familiar road. Images of Christ, for example, that we loved as a child may be a stumbling block to today's children. "God is like *this*" we may say, halting their exploration into the realm of the holy. The stereotyped repetition of traditional art may not enter the heart of a new generation and comic book art in recent curriculum trivializes the story. It seems reasonable to start afresh and make active research from an old art.

For example, consider finger painting.

"It is a remarkable paradox that the most ancient of art forms is relatively new and unexplored in the western world." So says the artist Mary Ann Brandt. Her painting glows with radiant color, sometimes reminding you of the energy present in a Van Gogh painting ... sometimes presenting recognizable objects that subtly emerge as faces and figures and visions. Other times the canvases seem to burst forth with a kaleidoscope of color. Imagine my surprise when I met this artist and discovered her media. She transports us into the numinous with fingerpaints.

But this is a kindergarten media you argue. Not so. Mary Ann Brandt explains how she began expressing herself in this media when attending a group that was exploring their dreams. Some in the group began to want a tactical expression and began to experiment with fingerpaints. After a few moments she was hooked. Her rules: choose colors that appeal to you at the moment. As your fingers move across the paper, the picture begins to take on a life of its own. Do not have a completed picture in your mind. Let the colors and your fingers lead you. "Sometimes I am surprised at what I have produced," she says.

As we seek to teach children about the unknowable nature of God, finger painting works as an appropriate media.

Begin your first class experiment in finger painting with a single color — black or blue — and let the children discover what strokes their fingers will create in the monochrome. The experience will gradually introduce its own sense of wonder.

Later give your class a Bible verse to illustrate. For example:

The heavens declare the glory of God. — Psalm 19:1

For with you is the fountain of life. In your light we see light.   — Psalm 39:9

20

Before the mountains were born or you brought forth the earth and the world — from everlasting to everlasting you are God. — Psalm 90:2

God is our refuge and strength, an ever present help in trouble. — Psalm 46:1

I lift up my eyes to the hills. Where does my help come from? — Psalm 121:1

Instruct your students to ponder these words. "Think about colors that express your thoughts. Relax and let your fingers move."

Mary Ann Brandt concluded: "Finger painting is more than kid stuff. You may discover something wonderful in the medium and in yourself as well."

Mary Ann Brandt's pictures can be viewed on the web site: www.fingerpaint.com with links to supplies needed.

Colors

The invisible God sometimes comes to us through colors. Sometimes in meditation waves of color wash over us. To prepare for this experience choose a color — such as blue. Catch the pure blue of a summer sky. Compare it with the blue of the sea, lake, pool. Look at the myriads of blue flowers from soft blue of bluebells to the deeper tones of delphiniums. Shut your eyes, remember and envision these tones of blue. Rest in these colors and enjoy the feelings that arise.

A surprising number of people see colors when they pray. Putting words and imploring aside they allow God to enter their prayers through colors. A feeling of deep peace arises as God comes to us through blues, indigoes, and violet tones.

A splash of red as you meditate is an energizing experience — a challenging experience of God — a feeling of passion and fire. Sometimes it evokes a feeling of sheer terror.

Sometimes we experience deep black. Just wait and breathe slowly. After a time, splotches of color will appear.

A yellow or golden light as we pray lifts the spirit. Again go to nature and its many shades of yellow: shiny buttercups, delicate primrose, deep mustard color of yarrow, or rays of the sun. Pale yellow tending to white is a clean and calming experience of God.

As we let our minds and thoughts dissolve into these shapes and colors there is no need for words. We concentrate on the colors and shapes which sometimes move like a kaleidoscope before our shut eyes. We absorb the feelings of these colors. Then, without words, we enter into a dialogue with mystery.

A beautiful stained-glass window captures these same meditation colors. Consider hanging a piece of stained-glass in your Sunday school window to catch the light — enticing the colors into your room.

Rainbows can dance in your Sunday school room by hanging multifaceted crystals in windows where they will catch the sunshine.

What joy there is in blowing bubbles. These lovely circles of transparency brilliantly reflect color and open our eyes to mystery.

Giving children the opportunity to create helps them learn something of the great creator God who said, "It is very good!" Mystery is at the heart of creativity.

The urge to create is a primal urge. Continue to consider new and different art media for your class to experience — making beautiful things to look at. The art of making paper flowers is popular in many cultures. Or consider creating sculpture from litter. Both of these methods cause us to look at creation with different eyes. More than objects used it's the interplay of children with these objects. The mind at play with materials it loves. The late Mr. Rogers of television fame tells the story of a sculptor who visited a neighborhood nursery school. The teachers, amazed at his ability to enthrall these active four-year-olds asked for his secret. He didn't overtly teach, Mr. Rogers answered, "He just loved the clay in the presence of the children. They saw and responded."

All the art forms — stained-glass windows, candles, silk flags, paints, crayons, pastels make it possible for us to create and it is uncanny the simple joy of living that comes from art creations.

Invite the children to share their creations and add their positive responses to other children's art. In Indian art it is not only the artist who gives form and content to a culture but also the *sagridaya* (the person of one heart) who knows how to share, to appreciate, and also to gently criticize because of an inner vision. Can your children become *sagridayas* for others in the class?

A Time To Reflect

Ponder art in your life and teaching.

1. Recall your first art experience. What did you create? Recall a time when you were amazed at what you could create.

2. Were you encouraged in art expressions as a child? Remember examples pro or con.

3. If you could create something beautiful in the world what would it be?

4. Consider the images you see on television and in the news. Then read Philippians 4:8. With what sort of images are you filling your mind?

5. As a teacher, look carefully at the images your class creates. In my fourth-grade Sunday school class boys often include guns and violence in the pictures they draw. How would you respond to this?

6. What is your favorite color? Do you know why you favor it? What associations do you have with this color? Can you recall a time when you were deeply affected by a color?

Clue 3
Symbols

As we consider the many things that call us to God and worship, one powerful item may be overlooked, especially in our work with children. That is the use of symbols. A symbol is something that points beyond itself to something else. In our case, we want to consider symbols that point to the holy. These are little shorthand messages from God and about God that abound in our daily lives and in our sanctuaries if we have eyes to see. These spiritual indicators are like signposts on the way. We seek to help our children become conversant in the language of these signs.

Here are two ways that symbols can enrich our work in promoting the spiritual growth of our children. First, they remind us of our biblical stories. Second, symbols can bring a theological, even abstract, concept down to a concrete recognizable example.

A fairly recent hymn "God Of The Sparrow" by Jaroslav Vajda illustrates both of these uses of symbols. Each phrase in the hymn contains something that reminds us of a Bible story or reference. In the first verse we sing: "God of the *whale*" which brings to mind the story of Jonah and we have the opportunity to find that story in the Bible and learn or recall it.

"God of the *sparrow*" reminds us of Jesus' words that God is mindful of every bird in the air. It echoes Psalm 84:3, "Even the sparrow has found a home...."

We continue to sing. "God of the *swirling stars*" is an opportunity to look at the creation story or ponder Psalm 8:3-4, "When I consider the heavens...."

Then, in the last phrase of the first verse we are challenged: How do you teach the concept of religious awe? And we realize that we already have been doing this — by considering the symbol of the tiny bird, the giant fish, and the boundless universe. Wonder, thanks, and praise are three elements of awe. God, who is the infinite mystery, becomes a little clearer to us through these picture words and Bible stories.

The remaining verses of this hymn teach such intangible religious concepts as God's judgment, reconciliation, redemption — all through symbols reminding us of Bible stories. These images from our biblical tradition are a rich resource for children.

You will find many hymns from your religious tradition that abound in rich symbolism. Just pointing these out or asking the children to discover them can enrich their worship and understanding of God. Recall that children today live in many worlds and are influenced by many images and symbols. We, as teachers, can help our children claim the symbols of the Christian community and grow in their understanding of what it means to be a Christian.

Tour Your Sanctuary

Ask your children, "What are the objects in your sanctuary that are religious symbols?" It would be time well spent to take your class on a tour of your place of worship, looking for and pointing out symbols. They will discover the richness of sacred signs. Arm yourself with a good book on religious symbolism before you begin your tour.

Undoubtedly there is a cross. Even this familiar symbol seems to have lost its meaning. An example of this was shared with me recently. My friend was in a jewelry store when a young couple walked in. Obviously in love, the young man wanted to purchase a gift for the girl. After looking around they came to the counter containing crosses. "How about a cross?" he asked. "That would be nice," the girl replied. He then asked, "Do you want a plain one or one with a little man on it?"

If we don't know the biblical story behind our symbols they become merely decorations. They lose their connection to God. A cross reminds us of the powerful crucifixion story and points beyond to illustrate the depth meaning of sacrifice.

Some of your children may wonder and ask, "Why do we have a lamb portrayed in our church?" "Why a ship?" "What do the letters IHS stand for?"

Each sanctuary will be unique in its symbols. Do you recognize the symbolic code language in yours?

As you continue to tour your church consider banners and the symbols they use and all other art forms you may find. Perhaps your church has stained-glass windows or woodcarvings or a baptismal shell, each with pictorial messages in symbolism.

Even ordinary objects in your church can become symbols that point to the holy. Is there a food box or object from a recent mission trip? Of which Bible story might these objects remind you?

There are layers of meaning beneath the surface image of symbols. I love the symbols that illustrate the unexplainable. My favorite is the *overflowing cup* for grace. I can think of no better way to express that gift from God.

A New Symbol

An alert teacher may want to watch for the emergence of a new symbol that helps your children feel closer to God — something unique to your group. Respect for traditional symbols shouldn't keep us from a reverent use of imagination and sensitivity in recognizing new ones. But be careful. A symbol is not a logo or slogan. Two questions to ask in watching for a new religious symbol are 1) Does it point beyond itself to the holy? and 2) Does it speak with power to where life is related? In a true symbol there is something unmanageable about the way it is formed. It seems to surface rather than being created. An apt symbol awakens the feelings and ideas symbolized without any further explanation. We are blessed to work with children who will shock us into new ways of seeing and thinking, and open us to new symbols if we are receptive.

As the children sing with awareness of the symbols in their songs and look at the symbols that surround them, they are nurtured and nourished and enriched through the awareness of the connection between God and themselves. Symbols help us play with deeper meanings.

Though the great infinite God cannot be seen or even totally grasped by our small minds, symbols remind us of the holy presence of God in our past, in our scriptures, and in our very midst. As we respond with thanksgiving, praise, and worship we allow the symbolic world to give us another level of experience.

A Time To Reflect

Think about symbols.

1. Right now, where you are sitting, look around you. What symbols do you see?

2. In your private meditation times, do you use symbols such as a candle or piece of sculpture or nature object to help focus your attention on God?

3. What symbols are in your classroom?

4. What is your favorite symbol? What does it do for you?

5. Take paper and pencil and just doodle for a few moments. What is your recurring doodle?

6. Think of a symbol illustrating what you would like to be like. What is it?

Clue 4
Music

For many people, their religious faith is closely tied to music. There is something about music that gives it the power to communicate and touch us in a multitude of ways. Perhaps it is closer than any other human expression in disclosing the relationship between the God of mystery and humankind. Music leads us to that essential encounter with God that enables us to move beyond ourselves. Lost in the sphere of music, though we may not be able to explain it, we sense something greater than ourselves.

One of the things that enhances Advent/Christmas most is music. Picture how dull the season would be without any music — no beloved Christmas carols, no joyful Christmas jingles, no bells, no trumpets, no glorious choirs. Some of our most powerful and beautiful music was written for the Advent and Christmas season.

As we consider the mysteries of God and the mysteries of the universe is anything more shrouded in mystery than music?

Researchers tell us that the musical instinct, the love of music, is not only a universal feature found in every known society, but is deeply embedded in multiple structures of the human brain and may be far older than previously suspected.

This desire to sing and rejoice is an exquisite pleasure and can usher us into God's presence. As we seek to challenge our students to open their minds to unanswerable questions consider with them this question: How do you think music first began? What was the very first song? Here are four ideas suggested by one class of children.

- The first song was a lullaby sung by a mother to her baby.
- It was a song of victory sung by an early hunter after killing a woolly mammoth.
- It was a song to placate the gods.
- The first song was a cry by a lookout to warn the tribe of danger.

Perhaps the first song was just a grateful expression of the delight in being alive in God's beautiful world.

If you asked your students this question, how often did they connect the origin of music with God? Whatever its source, music and song can bring us close to God.

Here's another mind stretcher to ask your students: Does God sing? What kind of song?

Zuzanne grew up in Western Europe. Her parents had no Bible or church connection but the home was filled with music. As a young child, Zuzanne was moved in a deep way by music. She grew up and became a violinist, playing some of the great classical music of the world. Her numinous experiences continued to grow through her music and she began to ponder the titles and subject matter of these inspiring pieces that she played. Finally, she found words for her feelings through the experience of Christianity.

When theological concepts are too difficult to grasp rationally, we can get a glimmer of understanding by singing. If we don't understand logically, we understand how it feels. For example: The glory of the Triune God finds expression in hymns like "Come Thou Almighty King," "Holy, Holy, Holy," or "Glory Be To The Father." These hymns articulate magnificent words coupled with an inspiring hymn tune. It is thrilling to hear these hymns booming forth on a powerful organ, lifting us into an ethereal realm of feeling beyond our mundane existence.

Music reminded one woman of her first numinous experience. As a very young child she always accompanied her parents to church services. When it came time for communion and the congregation began to sing the haunting communion hymns, a feeling would come over her and tears would flow down her cheeks. She didn't cry aloud or sob. She silently wept. She recalls she wasn't feeling sad, just deeply touched at a level she could not explain. The experiences remained vividly with her into adulthood. Continuing to reflect, she realized that she had known the incarnational reality of love and belonging in those services of worship.

In asking the question in workshop settings with teachers, "What do you think is the most popular hymn?" I was surprised to discover every time one or more persons answered, "Amazing Grace." There must be something about this hymn that triggers a deep response. "Grace" is one of those beautiful concepts that is difficult to explain logically but can be felt as we sing. Actually, the answer to the question is the simple song most of us learned as children, "Jesus Loves Me." Again a powerful concept that is accessible to us through music.

The Advent/Christmas season raises some deep concepts that can be experienced through music.

Consider Advent — the promised coming of Christ — the longing — the desire — the age-old waiting. The sense of waiting is thick. Something enormous is developing. Can we feel the mysterious thing that is coming? These feelings are picked up in hymns such as "Come Thou Long-Expected Jesus" and "O Come, O Come, Emmanuel." As we sing we experience the tingle of anticipation. Advent is a mystery we can't understand but we sing it.

The wonder and mystery of the actual birth enters our hearts through beloved songs such as "Silent Night" and "What Child Is This?" The mystic Hildegard said, "Jesus is the song of God. His birth brings harmony back into the world." The scriptures tell us that lacking words to describe that event, the angels sang. They sang of peace and joy that gave God glory. We still sing to express the amazement of that birth.

This is a wonderful time in our classes to hear and consider Christmas hymns from other cultures and countries that express these universal feelings: longing — desire — wonder — mystery — amazement — joy.

Perhaps our best teaching during this season is simply to enter the experiences through song ... to sing the mystery.

A Time To Reflect

Reflect on music in your life and teaching.

1. What kind of music do you prefer?

2. What song is running through your head right now?

3. What is the first music you can remember? Where were you? Who were you with?

4. Was music a part of your religious life as a child? If so, what song do you still remember?

5. Does your class have a favorite song? If so, what do you think makes it a favorite?

6. Jesus sang a song at the Last Supper. If you were at that Last Supper with Jesus, what song would you want to sing?

Clue 5
Sounds

Encounters with God occur in the NOW moment. If we are to experience God it must be now. The God of the past is learned about in stories and much of our time as teachers is spent in telling these stories. But even in listening to scripture our minds go back to hearing scripture in previous settings and we miss the impact of hearing it fresh now. Or some word or phrase projects us into the future with dread or anticipation and the present hearing is lost. Sounds help us engage in the moment and that is the clue we wish to follow in this chapter. While learning our stories is necessary for background, sound serves a different purpose. Like listening to music, no matter when it was created you appreciate it now. You experience the same nowness in which it was created. The use of sounds seeks to do the same thing — to engage us in this moment. Sounds bring us into the present and suddenly we are not just listeners but participants in the story.

As we seek to make the Bible stories fresh and powerful for our students consider setting an atmosphere, a background, for these stories by the use of sounds. Your students are probably familiar with the importance of background sounds and music in movies — building tension, anticipating danger, expressing joy. Try creating just such an appropriate atmosphere for our Easter stories. These stories have a strong aural accompaniment that we often miss because the stories are so familiar. This familiarity may have dulled our hearing. Sound can revitalize our experiences of these important stories and create a balance between inner meaning and its outer form.

Look at the following three examples:
* Jesus praying in Gethesmane.

    The teacher reads the story found in Mark 14:32-42 and asks for suggestions for sound effects from the class. They may begin by suggesting nature sounds — the sounds of the rustling leaves in the garden. This sound can be created by simply rubbing palms together or shaking tambourines or using wire brushes on drumheads. Identify the feelings in this story. Fearful anticipation, mounting tension, mystery — all are present. Keeping the feelings foremost let the class create the mounting tension. Perhaps one child will suggest the sound of distant footsteps approaching or the clinking of coins from Judas' money bag.

- Palm Sunday

The teacher reads John 12:12-13 and asks for suggestions. Palm Sunday is a natural for children's sounds. First identify the feeling — exuberant joy. How is this expressed? "Hosannah" may be a dated word for children. As the crowd watching Jesus approaches Jerusalem what modern sounds and shouts come to mind? Suggest this scene to your students: The stadium is packed. The basketball game is extremely close. As the fans cheer and the volume rises, the hometown team becomes energized and wins the game. Each individual is expressing himself/herself yet becomes part of a powerful instrument composed of many voices. There is a crescendo of sound — a focusing of energy. Can you capture this excitement as you read the Palm Sunday story? Jesus is coming — he is getting closer — he is passing by. Encourage the class members to be present at this moment with exuberance and excitement.

- Peter's betrayal

The teacher reads Luke 22:54-62. Ask: What is the feeling here? Consider despair — hopelessness. What sounds set the mood for Peter's agony in the courtyard? The class may want to begin with normal night sounds such as the sounds of a crackling fire. Perhaps a night wind blowing and then the crow of a rooster can add startling impact to this story that may be missed by a mere reading.

Experiment with creating the sounds from different parts of your classroom to gain different perspectives.

An added benefit of this type of experiencing scripture is that the non-readers in your class have an equal opportunity to participate. It is so easy in our teaching to rely solely on reading or telling our stories.

We are perhaps underusing a powerful tool when we neglect to consider other uses of sound as background to our Bible stories. Recall how the voice articulates sounds without literal meaning. Is anything more terrifying than a scream or more distressing than a moan or more joyful than a laugh? Yet — have you ever heard the above Easter stories accompanied by any of these voice exclamations? In addition, sounds have power by continuing to vibrate, echoing back like the wake of a boat.

Many sounds can be made with the voice. No other props are needed. We can sigh and cry, giggle and laugh, whisper or scream, hum or shout, grunt or gasp, boo or cheer. Ask the students to feel these sounds of their voices in their bodies. Notice how the different sounds feel differently as we seek to express a deep emotion. Allow the vibration of word and sound to enter the body and nurture the spirit.

Underlying, Universal Sound

There is another use of sound that you may want to consider as we seek to encounter God. At every single place and every different time there are sounds to hear and no two sounds are ever exactly alike. By concentrating, we can train ourselves to choose the sounds we hear. For example, birds singing above near-by traffic noise. In the same way we seek the wavelink on which the God who is all around us can enter our consciousness. Listen harder. Prepare yourself for the word of God. Just as we have to know what we are looking for before we can begin looking for it we seek to listen for God.

Can you hear a sound beneath all other sounds? There is a hum of energy behind all things — an unceasing note humming creation into being. It is a deep undertone to life. A humming that is reassuring and constant, "the mechanics of the universe" as one author described it.

How do you become aware of this sound? Anthony DeMello, in his book *One Minute Wisdom*, offers this advice: "Become an ear that gives heed to every single thing the universe is saying. The moment you hear something you, yourself, are saying, 'Stop.' "

Clothed in this aural fabric God may speak to you.

A Time To Reflect

Become aware of sounds.

1. Make a point this week of listening to the sounds around you. Why are some sounds so pleasant and some so jarring? Name the most pleasant and the most jarring sounds you are hearing.

2. What sounds energize you? When and where do you hear them?

3. Practice listening more deeply and open yourself to the invisible world of audible vibrations we call sounds. Time yourself for five minutes and listen to all the different sounds.

4. Put your thumbs in your ears. Shut your eyes and become aware of your own internal sounds — that strange, muffled thumping.

5. Consider the sounds in your classroom. They are creating a background — an atmosphere. Consider how music can alter the mood of your classroom. How are you taking advantage of this resource?

6. Have you ever had the experience like Peter of a sound recalling an experience that creates guilt?

Clue 6
Movement

As we continue our journey into the mysteries of God these words from an ancient mystic ring out: "Oh, God, who may well be loved but not thought" and usher us into experiences of movement. This method of teaching challenges the assumption that children can only know God when they can think and talk about him logically. Children know through their bodies.

The body can be used to express and explore otherwise inexpressible things. Children are better and freer in the uses of their body than most of us as adults. Some spontaneous movements are common to all children. They jump up and down when excited, crouch when afraid, fling their arms wide when they are happy and content. These movements come naturally and are untaught. As we age, we seem to stiffen — become more frozen and statue-like in our movements. This rigidity may extend to our theological ideas as well. Again, here is an area where the children can teach us. Agility and vitality are two gifts children bring.

The stirring up of love is one of our tasks as teachers. This can find expression through our physical bodies. How does it feel to know a God of love? A warmth? A fire? A surge throughout the body? A wild abandonment of joy? We can invite children to pay close attention to the messages from their bodies in the form of feelings and sensations. Bowing the head, folding the hands, perhaps kneeling without saying a word can remind us that we are in the presence of God here and now in our lives. These different and definite physical acts slow us down and open us to God.

Begin with breathing. Air and wind are familiar and powerful images for the Holy Spirit. Talk about wind. It is something children know and adults have too often forgotten, at least in its aspects of fun and beauty.

Do some breathing exercises alone or with your class. As you breath in think of a great light that grows brighter and brighter. As the air goes out imagine the world is being warmed with your light of happiness and love.

Choose one thing you love most. It may be a person, a parent, a pet, an interest such as music or a sport or God. Whatever you love most hold in your mind. Concentrate on that one thing. All thoughts are directed upon it. Breathe deeply and rhythmically letting the power of love flow through you and out into the world.

Then, filled with the spirit of love and God, welcome a new day. Stand tall. Take a deep breath and raise your arms overhead. Then stretch out your arms in welcome of a new day. Finally, bending slightly, swing your arms down behind you, palms up. Return to the beginning position and repeat moving rhythmically. Allow these movements to awaken something within the heart that is beyond words — a deep satisfying feeling in being alive in a new day — a bedrock feeling of joy no matter what the circumstances.

A yoga position called "Salutation to the Sun" uses every part of the body in twelve positions. Applying these postures or positions to the Lord's Prayer gives new understanding to the words.

Standing tall you begin:

- **Position 1:** Palms together in prayer position *(Our Father)*
- **Position 2:** Locking your thumbs, stretch your arms high overhead beside your ears; look up *(who art in heaven)*
- **Position 3:** Bend forward keeping your knees straight; look at your knees *(hallowed be thy name)*
- **Position 4:** Stretch your left leg back, your left knee on the ground; right foot remains bent between your hands; lean slightly forward and look up *(thy kingdom come)*
- **Position 5:** Move right foot back to meet your left foot, straighten legs to make a tent of your body, buttocks high in the air, head between your arms; heels of your feet gently pressing toward ground *(thy will be done)*
- **Position 6:** (This position is a tricky one) Your knees, chest, and chin in that order, come to ground; your pelvic area is kept a few inches off the floor; your fingertips are in line with your shoulders, arms are in close to ribcage and elbows point upward *(on earth)*

42

- **Position 7:** Lower your pelvis to the ground as your upper body slides forward; slowly raise your head, then your chest off the ground; try to rely on the strength of your back muscles, using your hands mainly to support the weight of your body *(as it is in heaven)*
- **Position 8:** Raise your body back into Position 5 — a tent *(Give us this day our daily bread)*
- **Position 9:** (This is a reverse of Position 4) Your right knee comes to the ground; try to bring your left foot up between your arms; lean forward and look up *(and forgive us our debts as we forgive our debtors)*
- **Position 10:** Move right foot forward to meet the left; stay bent at the waist; keep your knees straight as in Position 3 *(Lead us not into temptation but deliver us from evil)*
- **Position 11:** Begin to slowly raise your body, stretching your arms high overhead, locking your thumbs as in Position 2 *(for thine is the kingdom, the power and the glory)*
- **Position 12:** Lower your arms; place your palms together in prayer position as in Position 1. Shut eyes. *(forever. Amen)*

Though this may seem complicated, most children easily learn to do these postures. If possible, have someone demonstrate the complete body exercise. Then work on individual positions and phrases of the prayer separately with the exception of Position 6 and 7 which need to be practiced together.

As we praise God, we stretch our bodies upward. As we recognize our humble place in the universe we bend forward. As we implore God's help we kneel and look up. Every muscle in our body seeks to know and praise God, and our bodies become conduits through which spiritual insight may arise.

The feelings of this prayer may become, not just a mental flash but a full-body experience.

Hands alone can be used to express a feeling of God's presence. Have you ever noticed the stylized hand positions in Italian paintings before and during the Renaissance? In many of these pictures the thumb and index finger are connected. Its meaning is that the ego (the index finger) is bowing to God (the thumb) in unity and love. The gesture is called the kissing of the thumb and finger — a sign of love.

Another common gesture in religious paintings is the palm turned upward. This pose suggests openness and inquiry.

Sometimes we think childhood is a carefree time, but many children are burdened with guilt. They often have strong feelings. There are friends they like and enemies they don't. These feelings toward "enemies" can block their channel to God's love. By physically enacting we directly confront these feelings. Try this: Children sit with hands in lap, palms up. Ask children to imagine they are holding themselves in one hand and their "enemy" in the other. Instruct them to hold their hands outward and ask God to bless each with love. Then gently entwine the fingers as a sign of your willingness to be at peace and ease with this "enemy." Do this slowly and prayerfully.

The body can help us understand a Bible story in a new way. In reading the Bible we hear a story. How can we "get into" the story? We strive for the experience, not words about the experience. In the same sense that no one can swim just by reading the word "swim" we long for more than stories about Jesus. We long to be in his presence.

Use this game as an entry point to experiencing a Bible story. Divide the class into partners facing each other and play the game "Mirrors." One child does some physical movement such as patting his head or raising his arm. The partner facing him mirrors the identical movement. Continue this for a few movements and then swap and let the other child begin the movements.

Now read Mark 3:1-6.

Working in the same pairs, instruct the class to produce a piece of mirror movement which presents this story. One partner is the man with the withered hand. The other is Jesus, the healer. Start with the man's hand held tightly into his body. Jesus puts his hand in a similar position. Then Jesus slowly opens his hand. The man mirrors Jesus' movement.

Do this exercise in silence, seeking to produce a realistic mime. Does it look like the opening of something that has been closed and lifeless for years? The movement of the body and the hands invite us into emotional participation — woundedness focused on Jesus.

You can decide whether or not to comment or have the class comment on this experience. You certainly do not want to over explain it.

A Time To Reflect

Consider movement in your life and class.

1. Recall your childhood. What was your physical life like? Can you remember running just for the sheer joy of it? Did you swing or play on a see-saw? Try to remember the physical feeling. Did you skip? Hop? What physical games did you play? Who did you play them with?

2. Do you feel comfortable using your body in worship? In the privacy of your own home experiment with moving your body as an act of praise to God.

3. On a busy, rushed day try shaking your hands and arms to help release the day's accumulations of stresses. Did you have a sense of shaking off tension? Consider how this might be helpful in your classroom.

4. What is your level of comfort with movement in your class? On the scale of one to ten, one is very comfortable and ten is very uncomfortable.

Clue 7
Words

To name something is to acknowledge its existence. If children are having numinous experiences as I believe they are, we can give them words to express these visions. Though words and logic can never capture the nuances we can try with an airy net of words to contain them.

Children have a different dimension of seeing that is only partially accessible to adults, but they are, I believe, valid in their own right. It would only be out of great presumption that the child's religious experience would be devalued or discarded. However, keep in mind that often their visions run far ahead of their ability to express them. These visions are diverse, overflowing, endless, abundant beyond measure or may be a new way of seeing a very simple thing.

I love the story from our Native American culture that tells how adults who had lived first in caves learned to make tepees by watching children play with cottonwood leaves. The children stacked the leaves against each other and used little sticks to keep them from falling over. The old men watched, learned to make tepees, and changed the lives of the whole tribe, for now they could follow the buffalo and take their homes with them. The old people still say we should always watch and listen to children.

"God" is a word, just a word, for the supreme unknown. What is the reality for which the word "God" was created? Children seem to know the word God and I often wonder how they learned it and what it means to them. One child asked, "Who was God's mother?" I suggested to her that God came before. God never came into existence and never passes away because God's very nature is to exist; and then the Omnipotent God made something out of nothing. Do they have any idea what I am talking about? Do I? I keep hoping a child will explain this to me.

Defining God

To help children enlarge their definition of God try this:

- **Step 1:** Give them this statement: God is a being beyond which no greater thing can even be thought.
- **Step 2:** Tell them this story (taken from *The Song of the Bird* by Anthony de Mello): In the ant world it is believed that God has two stings whereas an ant has only one sting. The ants believed that in ant heaven they will also have two stings and they argue about where the stings will be located.
- **Step 3:** Children seem comfortable talking to animals, so begin here. Say to your students: Pretend you are a reporter. Your assignment is to talk to different creatures about how they see God. How might a cat think about God? A butterfly? A bird? Choose other animals that you think would be appropriate. Next, expand the reporting to humans. How would a three-year-old child think about God? What would God be like to a rocket scientist? To a brain surgeon? Add other appropriate suggestions.
- **Step 4:** Consider again the definition you gave them in Step 1. Perhaps the understanding that God is a being beyond which nothing greater can be thought, might be clearer to them now.

God is only a word to describe the experience. God is beyond our greatest desire or thought. It is startling to consider that we dare to give a name to this supreme being; this blinding light of the universe; this penetrating all-seeing eye; this infinite beyond our words. Using language to reach the unreachable sets a kind of limitation on us. God is above every name that is known.

Next, consider words about God. There is a difference between words that can be understood and words that are not to be understood but known. For example: God is love.

A little child told me a truth about God. Six-year-old Isaac was given the assignment by his teacher to write about himself. On a cheerful picture with bright colors of yellow and red with straight rows of tulips and a sun with a smiley face he wrote: "I am a happy child. I was made to be held."

Children know what love is. Can they make the jump that God IS love? Even though God is unknowable there is something in us that seeks God and knows we belong to God.

The love of God is no simple thing. Not only do we long for love, we long to be the most loved. One friend shared with me that as a child she was continually asking her mother, "Who do you love most — God or me?" The answer "I love you both" never satisfied her. How can we understand and help our children understand a love that knows no boundaries — no competition — no jealousness?

Words said over and over shape us. Consider the children's gospel song: "Praise him, praise him, all ye little children, God is love, God is love." If you do not know the tune, say the words in a clapping rhythm.
.
> *Praise him, Praise him,*
> *All ye little children,*
> *God is love, God is love.*

Eastern religions have taught us the power of mantras in helping us center on God. A mantra is an incantatory recitation said over and over working deep into the soul. Children might say "Almighty God" or "Amazing God" or "Loving God" over and over and slowly they find God is with them in the deepest level of their lives.

Along the same lines simple words like "Thank You, Lord" repeated inwardly over and over throughout the day can bring God closer. Or consider "Use me, Lord" or "Thy will be done." This really becomes a kind of inward prayer preparing us for God's wonder. John Westerhoff suggests that we say over and over "Christ is risen! Christ is risen!" rather than give an elaborate and oftentimes confusing explanation of resurrection.

To get your children in the habit of thinking about God throughout the day, set an alarm clock in your classroom to go off every ten minutes. Continue with your regular teaching plans for the day. When the alarm sounds stop whatever the class is doing and children silently say their one or two word mantra. Take only a few seconds, then continue with the class, following the same pattern through the entire class session. This is done so that they may be mindful and to counteract our perpetual tendency to forget about God. Encourage the children to get in the habit of inwardly praying to God while outwardly they continue with their regular schedules.

A Time To Reflect

1. Take your time and list all the names you can think of for God. Consider how each name is a little different. With what name for God do you feel most comfortable?

2. Consider other words that cannot be understood, but though not understood, are known. For example: happiness, joy, loneliness, grace. Can you think of others? Meditate quietly on these words.

3. Try using a prayer mantra yourself. Choose perhaps a favorite Bible verse such as "God is my refuge and my strength" repeating it often throughout the day.

4. In all of language what is the most beautiful word you know? Ponder your answer.

5. Think of the names of the children you love. When you know a name you recall the person behind the name. Say the names to yourself and reflect on the images that emerge.

6. "The best things cannot be said. This is why the second best are misunderstood." Ponder this statement and try to think of an example illustrating it.

Clue 8
Poetry

For some people poetry is a clue to the mystery of God. Just what is poetry? Before looking the word up in a dictionary try for your own definition. One of the best definitions I have ever read is "when words pause." Poetry is just prose broken up in lines so that you will pause as you read it and wonder. Poetry is perhaps, more than anything else, the communication of amazement before the fact of this phenomenal world. Something catches our attention. We pause and in expressing it — poetry is born.

As we think about the nature of God, poetry helps us ask the right questions. Questions about God are not scientific questions. They are not questions of logic and rationality. They are questions of wonder. One of the earliest poems a child learns is:

> *Twinkle, twinkle little star*
> *How I* wonder *what you are.*

That is one way we know God exists, not by the fact that we wonder but by the way of wondering. This is one of the great lesson children have to teach adults — to wonder.

Just last week I saw an example. At a health club, a little boy around four years of age was standing at the drinking fountain while his mother waited impatiently. As she urged him to hurry he looked up with wonder in his eyes and said, "But the water goes up — and then down — up and down." What a wonderful thing and all the adults had missed it.

Moments of wonder occur when with the openness of a child we see — as if for the first time.

Children are natural poets because they look. As adults we glance. Have you ever seen a young child enter a room of strangers and just look at everyone? No need to smile or be charming or say the right thing — just look, long and hard. Secretly, I have wished I could do the same. But a look makes us vulnerable. It opens us up. It is so intimate. We recognize looks of hate and they are frightening. On television we see faces full of hate, yelling, screaming, looking so ugly. A look of love softens the face. Looks of love are so affirming. We recognize goodness in the face of others.

I know a man who has made fifteen trips to the South Pole to "winter-over" and work sometimes three months and sometimes as long as a year. He says he has seen incredible sights there, and there is something in his mien — a look deep in his eyes of strength and a great inner stillness.

I knew a woman with compelling eyes who taught music. Her inner eye had seen something of infinite beauty through music. The expression from those azure eyes were unlike anything I had ever seen. Their visions have changed these persons. How blest they are.

As adults we seldom look at anyone. Children and poets look. In the same way God is saying to us: "Please look at me. I am all around you. Look at me and you will see so much love looking back at you. It is a precious thing."

God's presence is in all things and in every place. Wherever we go or wherever we are, God is present. The fact that we cannot see God causes us to forget this. Children teach us the sacred is right here and now. Through their wonder they help us see this sacred in the world.

Play A Game

Most children know the simple game "Where is Thumbkin?" Using that chanting rhythm, play "Where is God?"

Teacher: Where is _____? (name of child, such as Sarah)
Where is Sarah?
Child: Here I am. *(child stands)*
Here I am.
Teacher: Have you seen the Lord?
Child: Yes, I've seen the Lord.
Teacher: Where was that?
Child: In the _____ (example: flowers, smiles of friends)

Give the students a few minutes to think about these answers before beginning the game. Where might we see God all around us? Have them think about the seasons or their favorite nature object. Anything can become a touchstone for utter delight in the fact of being alive in the physical world. Participating in this game they are already thinking like poets.

Continue this game until the students are thinking "outside the box." The purpose here is broadening, not merely reshuffling stale ideas and cliché answers. Conclude this game by reading the story of Joseph and the ladder to heaven (Genesis 28:10-17). Memorize verse 16: "Surely the Lord is in this place and I was not aware of it."

Continue to develop this ability to pause and look and wonder.

Encourage your students' awareness through journaling. This can work for children as young as third grade but works best with older elementary or junior high students. As a Lenten discipline give each student a small notebook or journal and instruct him/her to record these two items every day:
- Something that surprises you
- Something that inspires you

Knowing you are going to write makes you more observant. There is an added acuteness to vision.

The goal is for each student to discover these surprises and inspiration individually but if keeping a journal is a new experience for your class, you may have to give them a jump start.

One way to do this is to divide the class into small groups and send them outdoors with the challenge of seeing which team can discover the most surprises and inspiration in fifteen minutes. While the hope is that the students will find surprises and inspiration in many places, nature is always a fertile field for ideas and a good place to begin.

After this scavenger hunt, the teams share their findings. In one fourth-grade class, for example, one team saw the surprise of a hawk trying to pick up a large limb and the inspiration of early spring flowers pushing up through frozen ground. Another team saw something that reminded them of the magic and fantasy they had seen in the movie *Lord of the Rings: The Twin Towers.* "It looked just like that — but tiny." And they were inspired by an unusual color in the sky that was "yellow like candles."

Students are encouraged to continue with their journals at home. The season of Lent is a time for turning inward and personal, spiritual growth. A private, unshared journal may serve best.

If students choose to share their journal they can report each Sunday during Lent.

In the following weeks, surprises were discovered by the same fourth-grade class by such things as seeing an old friend unexpectedly and finding inspiration in daily Bible reading. Nature continued to be a source of inspiration. The volatile weather at this time of year was the source of some surprises and inspiration. One student even found inspiration in spring mud, remembering the Genesis story that Adam was formed from clay.

Since writing is a catalyst for sharper self-observation and reflection, older students may wish to take their journals a step further by studying them for individual spiritual understanding. Ask them to look for answers to these questions:

- Is there a pattern in your discoveries?
- Where do you most often find surprises?
- Where do you most often find inspiration?

Understanding this about themselves they can return to these sources and choose to accent them. What we choose to see says a lot about who we are.

An old name for Lent is "enlightenment" and that is what we seek. As a teacher consider enriching your own spiritual life by also keeping such a journal.

The book of Psalms, which is a book of poetry, can help children look afresh. It can connect the mundane and holy in their everyday lives.

The British Benedictine, Sebastian Moore, is quoted in *Christianity Today* as saying, "God behaves in the psalms in ways he is not allowed to behave in systematic theology." This is good advice for us as we seek to move beyond a logical learning about God to an encounter with God.

Psalms do not deny our earthy feelings but allow us to reflect on them, right in front of God and everyone. This is especially good for young boys who are often turned off by constant cloying sweetness and a trouble-free view of life. By fifth or sixth grade, religion and poetry may seem sissified, silly, and unrelated to the world in which they live.

The psalms defeat our tendencies to try to be holy without being human first.

Try having your class write their own poem using examples from the book of Psalms. Don't be put off by unfamiliar words and allusions to unfamiliar things. The meaning and sound of strange words are often what makes it poetry. Because of the length of some psalms it is all right to only look at part of a psalm.

First find an idea in the psalm with which children can identify. Give the children a way to experience the main idea and feelings the psalm is expressing. Once they see what it is about they can write their own. You may need to give children some of the main ideas and feelings in the psalm. Try to connect to the children's feelings. Concentrate on that feeling — even magnify it. Don't rush. I found it took twice as long as I anticipated, but they were pondering. Surprisingly, the most active children took to this eagerly.

Here are three suggestions.

- Children enjoy thinking about God and how they can know God exists. A good place to begin is with Psalm 136. Repetition is natural to children's speech and much easier for them to use in expressing their feelings than meter and rhyme. After reading the psalm, discuss it with your class. The events listed are mighty and awesome in verses 1-9. Beginning with verses 10 through 22 it continues as an effusion of praise to God's presence throughout history. But look now at verses 23-26. The psalm becomes more personal. Ask the class to think back over the last 24 hours and list twelve events from their life ending with the refrain "His love endures forever" or, to bring it into the present moment use the refrain "God loves me." Perhaps an experience of God in the mundane of their lives will surface.

- Children know there is evil in the world and that it has power. Ask the children who the bad guys are in their computer games, on television, or in the movies. Ask: What makes them evil? Read Psalm 55:1-11. Talk about any words they do not understand. Ask: What images of terror and war have you seen? What thoughts trouble you? Ask them to list their thoughts using words they really use when they speak. Do they understand the psalm and connection to themselves? Talk about it. Honor their questions, responses, and experiences with integrity. Lift up common threads in their lives and this psalm. Does it remind them of anything they have seen on the news or experiences from their own lives? If the children have difficulty, beginning prompts may be necessary. Suggest: Things that scare me are _____. When I see gore and horror I _____.

  One eleven-year-old child said, "Things that scare me are movies or games with violence or graphic showings of blood. When I see gore my heart rate goes up and I close my eyes and wish the movie or show to end in happiness." These high-tech images are so riveting. They may penetrate and sear into the mind. Shocking, invasive material can over stimulate a young mind without a child having the ability to process and integrate it. Look with the class at how the psalmist concludes. Read verses 22 and 23. The recognition that God surrounds creation and that we are in God's hands is reassuring and comforting to children of all ages. Ask them to write their own poem.

- Children are aware and often have knowledge about other religious traditions. They live in a pluralistic world. Read Psalm 133. Allow questions about any strange custom or unfamiliar location here. As they write about a situation when everyone gets along, encourage metaphors they can come up with. One child wrote, "When everyone gets along it is like having a load of steel lifted off your head because you are not worried about being mad or getting even with someone."

Have they seen examples of children from different cultures getting along together or not getting along? One child shared with me a memory of a cruel racial slur she had heard one classmate make to another in second grade. When I expressed strong negative reaction, the child, now eleven said, "It wasn't her fault. She was too young. She was expressing her parent's feelings." Once again I learned wisdom from a child.

Limericks

Before we leave poetry, just for the fun of it, consider limericks. If methods don't work for you — if formulas fail — just how does a person become transformed internally?

Think about biblical visions and listen to children's insight about God. Then instruct children to write a limerick. The playful attitude unlocks deep thinking. The rhythm carries the thought.

Explain the limerick formula: It is a poem of five lines. Lines one and two rhyme; lines three and four rhyme and line five rhymes with lines one and two. These were written by a group of teachers:

Limericks On Transformation

There was a young lady from here,
Who knew her Bible quite clear.
Till zapped by the Spirit,
(She trembled to hear it)
Not words but grace brought God near.

There was a young man from this nation
Who sought inner transformation.
But try as he might
He was losing the fight
Till God's presence brought his inspiration.

"I'll be spiritual" the young man swore.
He tried methods and methods and more.
But alas he was miffed
To find Grace was a gift
Not a record of things tried before.

A Time To Reflect

Consider poetry in your life and your class.

1. What sparks your interest and causes you to pause and wonder? Think of one thing you have seen today.

2. Have you ever written a poem? Try using this method: First write a paragraph describing one or more of the students in your class. Write about the ones that matter most to you. Use language that is natural to you. Then break the paragraph up into poetry by arranging your sentences in different line formation. Can breaking a sentence in the middle enhance the meaning of both lines? Read it aloud. Look at the visual shape of the poem on the page. Create words that rhyme or not. You have just written a poem.

3. When have you experienced sudden unexplained epiphanies — little bubbles of joy that surface and disappear? Try to hold on to these sudden moments.

4. As you read the limericks, consider the transforming moments of your life. Consider writing a limerick. Here's a prompt — three words that might get you started: uncover, discover, recover.

Clue 9
Nature

Nature is a constant source of messages and surprises from God if we have eyes to see. At any time — everywhere — nature has the potentiality of revealing something of God to us. It is a common trigger for a God encounter.

The first assurance of God may come as we notice the predictability of nature. Day follows night. Summer follows winter. All things pass. God never changes. We can count on it.

In addition to predictability, spending time in nature enables us to sense the harmony, the interaction of all the elements and forces of life and gives us a sense of unity. There is an incomprehensible feeling of oneness in nature. Adults, in struggling to explain a numinous experience from childhood, talk of a feeling of connectedness, an overwhelming feeling of being a part of a larger whole, of seeing themselves woven into the tapestry of life.

A third affirmation of God comes from noticing the infinite, creative abundance all around us. The beauty and power of nature is so exquisite and boundless it strikes us with terror and awe. All canyons and forests and oceans and mountains and flowers and foliage, boundless and beautiful, complicated and simple. There is always more — so much more — and we meet the divine mystery at the core of the universe. Nature is capable of bearing the weight of mystery.

Work in some plan to go outdoors and have unstructured time in nature with your students. There are many places for your class to gather outdoors: church yard, a local park, farm or beach, a nearby yard. The purpose is to invite children to notice and describe what they experience without initially having to do anything with it. Care needs to be taken to allow children to interpret experiences for themselves. Invite them to raise questions as to the meaning of images they see, and affirm it all. The important thing is to help them accept the integrity of their experiences before translating it in your own interpretation.

There are many things in nature that invite us to observe some of the mystery of God. Include some simple experiences. For example, if you live near a wooded area:

- Sit or lie down in the shadow of a tree. Read Psalm 36:5-7.
- Look for trees that have been broken and damaged by storms. Look for signs of new life from the old. What insight or questions do students have?
- Inspect branches, leaves, trunk, and roots — just look.
- Look at a tree stump. The rings of a tree tell its age. Count the rings.
- Study shadows. Read 1 Chronicles 29:10-18.
- Look at small things. Buds and shoots that show so little strength and promise at first but will crack concrete or cause a rock wall to crumble. Can anyone find an example?
- Notice trees with seeds hanging on them or lying on the ground. How do they travel?
- See how many varieties of plants you can discover. Notice the diversity of colors, sizes, shapes, stem formation, and leaf placement. Look closely at a flower.
- Experience rain. Read Psalm 65:9-13. Enjoy fresh rain smells. Smell is a powerful access to God in nature. Notice the smell of damp moss or ferns. Also be aware of the sounds made as raindrops strike different objects.

In the above examples sometimes scripture is suggested. In others, asking the right question can help direct their thoughts. Experience these simple things as mysteries. Deep, direct experiences of nature awaken a sense of wonder. Children expand beyond their own little worlds. These spiritual moments are direct, personal, and often have the effect, if only for a moment, of waking us up and expanding our understanding of who we are and our place in the universe. Choose experiences that suit your landscape. Perhaps water-related experiences are more suitable for your class. Just create simple experiences that uncover a child's openness and directness of perception.

Hopefully, questions and wonderings will arise from these experiences. Often, when a child asks a question, his question reveals a broad sense of wonder about God's action in the universe that goes beyond a simple answer. Good and evil — beautiful and ugly — are seen. These may raise some questions. Can they discover examples of chaos and ugliness out of which comes beauty and strength? We might try to answer their questions but in doing so we probably are missing the point. It is more important for you to focus on the sense of wonder behind the question and encourage children to explore it together.

Haiku, a poetry form from Japan, might be a helpful way to reflect on these experiences. Haiku takes children into the rich world of imagery and interpretation. It offers snapshots, both simple and complex, as a child's own perception might be.

Strict rules in writing haiku help a child condense the essence of the experience. It contains three lines. The poem contains a season word like summer or winter or a symbol of the season like snow or buds. The first line has five syllables, the second line has seven syllables, and the third line has five syllables. An example:

> *I see autumn trees*
> *Heavy with tight hanging seeds*
> *Life will come again.*

The best haiku makes you think and wonder for a lot longer than it takes to say it. One should try to create freshness in subjects taken from daily life.

Sometimes nature can give us a new interpretation of a Bible story.

For years I tried to add marsh marigolds to my wildflower garden. I loved their glossy, shining, perky, expectant blossoms. I studied them and finally got a beginning plant. They like "wet feet" so I carefully planted them in neat containers of wet soil and then covered the container with rocks and placed the container by the run-off from the drains at my house. The flowers bloomed and were just as glorious as I remembered when first seeing them in the wild — a verdant, vibrant clump of gold by a mountain pond.

Then one day I discovered several small plants had jumped out of the tub and were growing in the boggy soil of the drainage ditch. Knowing that they would dry out and die I dug them up and returned them to their container. But soon others had also escaped the confinement of the tub. Whether these were the same plants or others I don't know. Now I just leave them. How they got out and why are mysteries to me. I don't know the answer and I can only live in the mystery. The marsh marigolds challenged me and came to mind later as I was reading the story of the prodigal son (Luke 15:11-32). I remembered the son's returning. The marsh marigolds caused me to wonder: Did the son leave again later? Was he looking for that same something even though he knew now there were consequences? Is life one continual meeting of challenges — searching for answers — facing temptations over and over? Do we continue to be prodigal until at the end we meet God?

In talking to adults about moments they felt the presence of God or the weight of unanswered questions enter their lives, time after time people would say, "I was staring up at the sky one night ..." or "Lying outdoors on my back as a child...." The vastness of the universe stretches our minds and thoughts. All that we know and don't yet know. The old/new eternal mystery is always there. One man shared, "Then I felt I was special and there was a special place for me. Looking up at the sky everything seemed perfect and connected."

Unfortunately, children seem to be doing less stargazing now. In addition to television and computers, excess lighting may be a cause. Light pollution has increasingly cut off children from their heritage of a dark star-filled night sky.

If it is possible on a night when you can see stars, go outdoors and lie down looking into the heavens with your class. One way is with heads together and bodies radiating like spokes of a wheel. Instruct the students to open themselves to God.

An exercise I wrote for my book *Planting Spiritual Seeds* (Abingdon Press, 1994) works well as a follow-up to this experience.

Each student creates a *quartos* book. Tell the students that since our logical minds cannot grasp the vastness of the universe, we will use our imaginations.

Give each student a large piece of typing paper. Instruct them to fold it in half and then in half again to make four pages. On the first page write: "I went out to meet God in space and _____."
On the top of the second page write: "Then _____." At the top of the third page write: "And then _____."
On the last page write: "Finally, _____."

Tell the students to use their imaginations to fill in the blanks. They are to limit their writing to the size of the page. This will help them condense and bring together their thoughts. To start their writing you might suggest:

- Imagine leaving the earth altogether. What would that be like?
- Imagine coming to the stars and beholding their orderly array. What would that be like? Push your imagination to the stars beyond known galaxies.
- Imagine coming to the immovable power beyond the stars, which guides and controls all things. What would that be like?
- Imagine coming to a place that is unchangeable, a place that is eternal, that exists in its own right.
- Imagine going outside of time, even beyond time itself — beyond anything that ever was. Who would you meet and what would you say?

Instruct the students to put something of themselves on the paper — their ideas, their imaginations, their personalities. Share these stories.

A Time To Reflect

1. Do you currently nurture a plant? What is it? How did this come about?

2. Complete this list. This is what I learned of God from nature:

3. What were your nature experiences as a child? Did you spend much time outdoors? Why or why not?

4. Do you currently enjoy nature activities such as gardening or hiking? If so, which activities? If not, why not?

5. Have you ever had a nature experience with your class?

6. What do you think your students wish for when they see the first star of the night? What do you wish for?

Clue 10
Sacred Space

Can we find a clue in a location? Scattered over our entire planet are sacred sites where people have sought communion with God. These mysterious, awesome places exert a powerful spiritual impact — places that impart a holy essence. Consider some of these. There are the mysteries felt in places like Stonehenge and Delphi where far back in the mists of time people came to worship. These places fire the imagination and keep their secrets. There are enigmas enshrined in places like Chartes Cathedral and Easter Island. They still hold this powerful essence of awe and unite us with pilgrims throughout the ages. We still seek this awesome God.

Stories and pictures of ancient sacred sites may arouse the curiosity of your children and plant seeds of interest. Who built them? For what purpose? How did some disappear and why? Of course stories and pictures are never the same as actually experiencing the overpowering sense of peace, wonder, and amazement of these places. Seeing the silver shimmer of waves on the Sea of Galilee or the flower-covered hillside setting of the Sermon on the Mount move us into a different level of understanding and communion with God. What can we do as teachers to expose our students to these mysteries? On this shrinking planet where more people and younger people are traveling worldwide, we can tell the stories that help prepare them for such experiences. We can whet their desires to see such places — to walk in these paths — to gaze on these wonders, in some cases, to touch these sacred shrines — to look and puzzle. We can develop appreciation for the instinctive, urgent, longing desire to commune with God that has been present in people and cultures through all ages.

Sometimes the appreciation of a sacred space and sensitivity to the story is in our own interpretation. Once, by chance, my husband and I were alone at the bank of the River Jordan just at sunset. I waded into these sacred waters — rays from the setting sun emblazed the sky and approaching above me was a white bird. The power of the story of Jesus' baptism overwhelmed me until my husband, with deflating realism said, "It's just a seagull." We laugh over this story today but I still remember the feel of water and the look of the sky. I am glad I knew the story as background for the experience.

Closer To Home

As intriguing and mystifying as these far away places are, the good news is that not all sacred places are at a distance in time and space. There are places in your own community like woodland chapels, magnificent sanctuaries, vesper points, and lovely gardens that envelop us in a sense of *presence*. All churches exert an atmosphere. Have you ever entered a church and been enveloped in a sense of peace and experienced a prayerful aura? Good vibrations generated by prayer seem to persist in a place. You feel the place is somehow sanctified. Go into your own place of worship when it is empty and you are alone. What are your feelings?

What Is Possible Today?

The spiritual can be revealed not only by traveling to some distant place but in many local areas as well. For example:

Many young people have their first experience of a numinous God at an outdoor evening vesper service.

Consider the model of a campfire circle at church camp. There is something provocative and feeling of "other" in this ancient circle setting.

A beautiful garden may be an inspiring possibility — a place where you meet God.

In Our Classrooms

Can we be in the presence of mystery in a classroom? The two seem incongruous. Yet that is our challenge.

Having a sacred spot in your church school classroom may seem a weak substitute for visiting a sacred place but it is possible.

If you are fortunate enough to have a large room consider adapting a corner for such a purpose. Begin by asking your students: "Is there a place that you can see in your mind that feels safe and peaceful? Shut your eyes and imagine such a place. As we visualize quiet places we find the quiet place in ourselves to match. Now let's try to create such a place here in our classroom." Ask the students to think in an interior way, to be inventive. If you have studied sacred places, what of their essence can you bring into your room? Suggestions might include a cave environment or chapel or forest glade. A tent-like structure in one corner of your room is a possibility. A place for tranquil silence perhaps with soft cushions to sit on. A screen or curtain might set off your sacred space. Create an area as clean and uncluttered as possible, alluring the soul rather than enlivening the mind. Consider white for your dominant color, or a soothing blue or mauve or lavender.

As far as possible, reserve your space for the purpose of prayer and meditation only. Good vibrations will persist in that place if the class makes a serious attempt to pray and meditate.

Use Of The Space

Go into the space for quiet prayer time — a time to allow the students to be silent and do nothing. Ring a bell or strike a chime three times to add to the power of ceremony that helps mark this as a special time and place. Listening to the resonance of the bell or chime as the sound dies away deepens the silence.

Encourage the students to feel peaceful and to rest. Imagine being held in God's arms. Experience the power of moods that affect our environment and each other. The students can become calm and feel more peaceful. The mind is clearer.

"But" you may argue "our Sunday school hour is too short as it is. There is too much to cover — to learn — to create. There is not enough time just to be." Yet here in this tranquil silence, these moments of quiet being, of putting the brakes on our speeded-up lives might be their best opportunity to experience God. Moments of wonder occur when we just let ourselves be. Our students can slow down, find their contemplative center, and experience a new way of being in the world. These moments give us an opportunity to support the emergence of an interior life with its particular energy and possibilities. Ring the bell again to signal that the time is over and allow them to return slowly to the active world.

If the Sunday school hour is just impossible is there another time — before or after Sunday school, or at some point during the worship service?

Altar

If the corner of a room is impossible consider an altar. An altar can be created in any place — a window ledge, a tabletop, a bookshelf. It can become a place of spiritual focus. A place which makes you want to stop, pause, ponder, and reminds us at a glance to say a prayer. Put on the altar things that speak to the heart: a candle, an ancient or interesting rock, a piece of old driftwood, a lovely piece of pottery, a flower, an ancient prayer shawl, a picture, a bowl of water with colored pebbles in the bottom, a sprig of evergreen reminding us of life eternal, anything that will invite your students to consider the mysteries of ancient times and sacred places and turn their thoughts to God.

In Russian orthodox spirituality there is a concept known as *poustina*. *Poustina* can be either a physical place, a retreat, or a secret place inside you.

Encourage the finding of a *poustina* for your students.

A Time To Reflect

Consider scared space — your own and in your class.

1. Do you have a special place in your home where you go for personal meditation?

2. Do you have accessories that help you focus on God — such as candles or flowers or aromas? What are they? Look around you — even a ticking clock can remind you that you have life to live now. Ponder how these accessories can turn your thoughts to God.

3. Is there a sacred place you like to visit or dream of visiting?

4. What problems would you face in creating a sacred space in your classroom?

Clue 11
Koans And Miracles

Ambiguity and unanswerable questions abound in this way of teaching. In this chapter we will consider some of these.

A koan is a mystery without any answer. It is affirming the words of Isaiah 55:8: "For my thoughts are not your thoughts and my ways are not your ways." We are use to logical, rational thinking but there are mysteries in life without any answer. We will never know the complete answer to some questions.

Many times our teaching in the church seems to be a concentrated attack on the lost realms of wonder and terror and ambiguity. But how can we explore the mysteries of God without coming up against these things? Skirting facing these issues only diminishes faith; for just to explore the unanswerable affirms our life. The seeking itself is fulfilling and not just what is sought. We are recognizing a deep yearning to question and explore — to imagine beyond what we can see — to be open to the magical in the everyday. Living your life believing in mysteries and miracles makes life an adventure.

So how do we teach? Our teaching is mostly showing what has been done and felt and experienced before, telling our stories over and over. We don't cease from doing this but our purpose is not so that they can be copied exactly but as a foundation and bedrock for new experiences. Can we prepare a place to welcome, to receive, and to encourage new exploration in the spiritual realm — even in our Sunday school rooms? All that has preceded us is available as a foundation — a reference point. These are our stories about God and I cannot overemphasize the importance of having this foundation. The natural imagination of children needs to be fed with images that have the possibilities of becoming spontaneous expressions of insight about God.

To move from the narrow path of "correct answers" and reciting of past explanations, give your students this assignment:
- Write three questions for which you think there are *no* answers.

- Gather the questions and mix them up.
- Distribute. Each student tries to answer the questions he/ she received in the swap.

Afterward consider: There are some questions we will never answer. We just live with the question. Sometimes, much later, an answer or at least an understanding of the question may surface. In archeology sometimes things long buried in the earth will surface, will just wick up, giving hints of a hidden culture. Approach these questions in the same mind set. Just let them work deep inside you.

Some of our churches have been guilty of constricting us in a culture with little room for ambiguity. We trivialize by reducing these enigmas to rational explanations. God is not a scientific explanation. Annie Dillard asks: "Does anyone have the foggiest idea of what sort of power we so blithely invoke?" We seek to prepare the minds of our students to how vast this understanding is.

In the light of this, let's look at miracles. What about miracles and the stories of miracles in the Bible? We do not have to go far in any major religion to run up against miracles. One of our tasks is to help children appreciate that which cannot be explained. Anthony de Mello says, "We are so enamored of the truth of history that we miss the truth of mystery."

It is important if we are trying to teach a child about miracles that we are open to believing in them, too. Often we want to explain the miracle away. Yet stories of miracles are keys to our faith. We, as teachers, need to foster our own sense of wrestling with what is hard to understand and be willing to surrender to the mysteries of God that we don't understand. We need to be open to the questions and not jump in with pat answers. Children seem more ready to accept a story at face value than we are. Again, they can be our teachers.

Our world is becoming more and more pluralistic. Other religions have broken in upon all but the most remote and sheltered communities. Other faiths have their own miracle stories. Our children may hear the Hanukkah story from the Jewish tradition, of the miracle of the flask of oil miraculously lasting for eight days, or the miracles from the Muslim belief that the Arabic Quran that exists today contains substantially the same Arabic that was transmitted to Mohammed and many more miracles from other cultures and religions. In considering these it is important for families of faith and our task as teachers to ensure children have a solid grounding in their own religion but at the same time not to make judgments about others. No easy task.

Teaching children that God created different nations, faiths, and cultures helps children learn respect for the miracles and stories of other faiths. We are all attempting to explain the great mysteries and wonders we see. There is and always has been a lot about the world we live in that doesn't make logical sense. Can we teach children to appreciate what can't be explained? If we are teaching in the church, chances are our particular church and its beliefs are, for us, the avenues to God and love. We try constantly to demonstrate this but also live with respect for another's point of view. There is never a need of violence over differences. In a nutshell, we want children to believe in the miracle stories of our religion, warn them against believing in false ones, and show respect for those of other faiths. Often the best way is simply to tell our stories and let them work their own power.

Sometimes life requires us to suspend belief. The world may be quite different from what we believe it to be. Truth is not only historical but mystical as well.

In thinking about miracles there is a danger that we are implying that we need to have a sky-rending revelation like Paul experienced on the road to Damascus to have a God encounter. Something dramatic — miraculous — outside the normal realm. This is not so. Many God-encounters are brief illuminating moments, tiny daily miracles, and these are emphasized in this book.

But we don't want to be guilty of the other extreme either — thinking that dramatic miracles do not continue to happen. Pattie Mattozzi, an artist and writer living in Texas, allowed me to share her story with you. This story, which until now she only shared with a few persons, happened when she was a child. In her words:

77

While living in Florida in Key Biscayne, I became seriously ill with polio at the age of five. Walking home from kindergarten I noticed I was having difficulty breathing. I could hardly walk. I was fortunate to arrive home safely but immediately collapsed on my bed with a high fever. I was delirious for three days and during that time was transferred to several hospitals in the greater Miami area. The diagnosis was polio. After my fever and severe headaches subsided I was weakened and paralyzed. I could use my arms but my legs wouldn't move. I was sent to the Children's Variety Hospital and remained there for almost a year. I needed constant care and attention as well as physical therapy. I remained cheerful throughout the ordeal even though I was no longer in contact with my family. I was placed in isolation for a considerable amount of time. Many children were in serious condition and required the assistance of iron lungs to aid in their breathing. The noise from the machines made it difficult to sleep at night.

Prior to my illness I had attended Sunday school every week and although I was small I had great faith. When I was taught of Jesus, I was absolutely delighted to know that someone as loving and fine as he, existed. Interiorly I had a supernatural confidence, a feeling of "well being" and security. I was amazed at his miracles, his love and kindness.

The weeks turned into months. My physician no longer had words of encouragement. On several occasions, I was placed on the floor with the entire staff watching to see if I could crawl. Once an attendant placed a banana on the floor several feet from my reach. I couldn't move. I was humiliated. Late that night I cried for the first time since my confinement. I wept hard, painful tears. I called for Jesus to come and make me well just as he had for the multitudes, centuries ago. I was weary of wearing diapers and sleeping on my back in a small steel bed with high bars like a prison. I fell asleep and had a marvelous dream. Jesus came to me and knelt down. He gently took my right hand and placed his arm around me. I put my left hand around his back. It was so vivid, so real. He was beautiful and the love and peace he brought comforted and strengthened me. He pointed to the darkness that was before us. As I turned and looked I could see nothing for it was a thick darkness. He began to talk and told me I was to return. As he spoke I looked closely at his face. I didn't want to leave. Here in this moment was the essence of life itself. I held in my arms heaven's greatest treasure.

I awakened around 3 a.m. feeling peaceful, strengthened, and loved. For some reason I had the idea to sit up and I did so! For the first time in months I was not lying on my back. I reached down and untied my feet that had been fastened into little shoes that were attached to the foot of my bed. The night nurse came in and was stunned to see me moving about. That morning there was great excitement in the ward. Everyone came in to see me! One of the physicians on duty lifted me to the floor and to everyone's amazement, I could stand, then I took my first step.

I was discharged late that afternoon. The drive home was engraved in my memory forever. I was released, set free. The world never looked so beautiful. My mother had fixed up my little bedroom for my homecoming. It was so pretty and neat with lots of new things here and there. As soon as I could, I slipped away. I went outside barefooted and felt the cool grass beneath my feet. It was a glorious summer day. I lifted my arms to heaven, thanked Jesus, and pledged him my life.

The remainder of that summer and on warm nights throughout the year I would take the screen out of my bedroom window and climb a tree up to the tile roof. There I would lie on my back and look at the stars and remember when Jesus came. This was our secret meeting place. Just he and I. It was dark on the roof, similar to when I met him. Often I would see a star fall and felt that Jesus had sent me a kiss. I would return to my little bed, comforted and strengthened, full of love and peace and ready for the new day.

For Pattie one defining experience crystallized the person she would become and the life she now lives.

These moments may still be occurring in the lives of our children. Open our eyes to your mysteries, Lord.

A Time To Reflect

1. In the privacy of your home consider the miracle stories of your faith. Perhaps you will want to read some of them again from your Bible. Consider some of the miracles of Jesus which were symbols of power used for the sake of goodness. For example, the story of the loaves and fishes, stilling the storm, walking on water, and the resurrection of Lazarus. List some favorites of yours here.

2. Do you have a true miracle story from your own life, or has anyone ever shared a miracle story from their life with you?

3. We frequently hear miracle stories through our news media — stories of miraculous escapes from disasters, and such. What do you think keeps you from believing them?

4. What part did fairy stories or fantasy stories play in your childhood?

5. How do you deal with miracle stories from other faiths in your teaching?

Clue 12
Death

Death will always be the archetype of the unknown. Can death itself be a clue to understanding the mystery of God? Here we have the opportunity to stress the importance of our theology and faith as the context out of which we deal with hard questions. Teaching about death is an individual subject. It is unique for each of us. First and foremost is for us to come to terms with our own beliefs about death. Review your own thoughts on this subject. Take a good hard look. This self-examining about your own beliefs is crucial. There are lots of things we'll never know. It's like a puzzle with missing pieces. Please don't try to teach something to children that you don't believe. Honesty is essential because first and foremost you can't fool children. They will know it if you teach something you don't believe. A wise teacher frequently says, "What do you think?" You will then avoid sermonizing, philosophizing, or giving answers that do not relate to what the child wants to know. Don't be afraid to say "I don't know." With older children I say, "I'm trying to understand that, too." Don't teach anything they have to unlearn as adults.

Now — if you have come to terms pretty much with your own beliefs are you all set? Unfortunately, no. This is one of the hardest things about teaching. Though it is crucial to study and come to terms with what you believe, there is a tendency to tell too much. Just engage questions your students are asking.

In addition to "when children ask" is there any other way we can help children? At the time of death is an appropriate time to make yourself available to a child, or in anticipation of a specific death. Our first tendency is to give a cliché answer we think will sooth a child. "She has gone to sleep," "God wanted her to be with him," "She is in the sky with a pair of shining wings," or "God needed him." Think carefully before you give these answers. Try to put yourself in the child's place. What are they really hearing you say? They might think "I'd better not go to sleep." Or "What if God needs me?"

Be open to learning from a child. Deep thoughts frequently come from the uncomplicated thought patterns of a child.

As teachers we have the task of answering questions concerning the facts of death such as: What is a funeral? What happens to the body? We can also help children deal with the feelings death produces.

Children should not have the reality of death concealed from them. All things die. Death is loss, but love is not. You can never lose love. You may lose the person or pet or object through which you know love. You will lose them but you can never lose that love — never. Whenever we do something or are with someone, pause and ask yourself: Is death a dreadful thing because it deprives me of this? But — no matter what — love of that person or situation will remain. We can accent it now and never lose it. Children need reassurance of this unending love.

Death involves fear and courage. We fear the unknown and death is the ultimate unknown. Paul Tillich said, "As humans we are aware of our existence and its finite nature." That's scary. We may be scared to death of death. It takes enormous courage to believe in life in the face of death — love in the face of hate — day in the dark of night. There is no need to sugar-coat this fear of death but face it with the children.

When you are leaving a birthday party what are children taught to say? "Thank you. I had a very good time. Thank you for inviting me." Can this be your attitude toward death? Picking up this theme, think about a death day party to give or to attend. Who will you invite? The people you invite can be all the people you have loved and have brought fun into your life. They can be a wonderful mixture of living and dead — past and present. What gifts are they bringing you? Some you may not like as much as others but gifts they are, nonetheless. Open them. Untie the ribbons. Beside each invited person list the gifts they bring and be thankful. What games will you play? List your favorite games and who you play them with.

This also reminds us to have a good time before we leave this life. Enjoy the games. Enjoy the birthday cake. Enjoy the other people who have come, bringing you gifts and say "Thank you." It is possible to praise God for everything.

Sometimes when something is too great to understand we tell a story.

A Fable

Just suppose it all began like this — a great meeting of souls was held in heaven. All angelic creatures, all unborn souls came before God.

And imagine this — to this awesome assembly God spoke, "I have something to show you. Here before you is my grand plan — the big picture." And there it was — in such great splendor and radiance that the audience gasped. It was beautiful beyond anyone's imagining. It was glorious beyond anyone's dream. The beauty of it was so exquisite it struck them with terror. There was the whole creation of history and the worlds. "You will see" God continued, "it is made up of many billions and billions of pieces. You are to choose one and live a life on earth that will help complete the picture. Some of you may choose to be great warriors and fighters. Some may choose to have wealth and talent. Some will choose to travel a difficult path. Some may choose to be tortured and abused. Some will have a long journey. Some will have a very short one. Some may choose a quiet hidden life. All parts are necessary."

Now imagine there was great buzzing among those assembled. Finally one soul spoke, "But what if we can't do our part? What if we fail?"

"Ah, then," said God, "this part of the picture will be empty until someone else comes along and fills it. It will eventually be filled. But each of you will be given all you need to succeed."

"How will we even know if we fail?" another soul spoke.

"You will not know until the end."

For a long time — ages and ages — these unborn souls studied the choices. They looked at where each life fit into the grand picture. They considered the span of history. They weighed the pros and cons numbering the challenges, and the possibilities of each life.

Finally, they all chose exactly what they wanted. Each understood the importance of their role. Each was filled with joy and excitement over the unique possibilities that were theirs.

Then God spoke again. "This ultimate picture will be forgotten when you go to earth. It will be the duty of each of you to try to remember it. There will be many temptations to help you forget. Satan has many tricks and lures. He will try very hard to get you to forget how beautiful the grand picture is — how important your section is to its completion."

Now imagine — if you will — that you were one of those souls and your carefully chosen choice is the very life you are living now. Try to remember why you made this choice. Why it was just right for you. Try to recall the joy you felt as you left heaven with your assignment.

This fable is not to preach pre-destination but to help children be grateful just to be alive in this life and also be willing to grow and change to fulfill God's purpose as it unfolds.

We are part of a divine plan in which we may not see the whole picture — always believing nevertheless, that in unhurried serenity the eternal is at work in the midst of time triumphantly bringing all things to pass.

A Time To Reflect

1. What do you expect from death?

2. Recall your first awareness of a death experience. Where was it? Who or what was it? How old were you?

3. As a child was there any adult who helped interpret your first death experience? Was this interpretation helpful or harmful?

4. Did you attend a funeral as a child? Try to remember your feelings at that time.

5. Do you have a Bible verse, a prayer, or a hymn that you would want to say when you are dying? How might you help your students find these sources of strength?

6. What words would you like as your epitaph?

Postscript

Have we discovered any answers in our following of clues — our probing of mystery? Have we lured children, or been lured by children, to look at life more deeply? Through the eyes of children we may catch a glimpse — a small lifting of the veil — that separates this world from the next, but in the end, as we attempt to understand and explain, it all comes down to stories and miracles. Stories that we can grasp because they build on human experience, and miracles because miraculous things still occur for eyes able to see.

In this book we have attempted as leaders and teachers to provide clues by telling faith stories — our own and those from the Bible. We have considered settings. We have explored different ways of knowing, such as music, art, and movement. We have looked at interpreting new experiences as understandings of the human/divine relationship. We have encouraged searching. We have tried to provide that unexpected question, observation, or perhaps silence.

But all of this is not the same as giving children faith. Faith is a deeply personal response to the experience of God's grace. With all our attempts there is always more — much more. Some questions are larger than any answer. It is our privilege to explore these mysteries with and through the eyes and innocent trust of children. We appreciate their playfulness, their vitality, and simple joy, and we watch them for new ways of being surprised by the sacred.